THE WILLOW
AND THE
BRIDGE

THE
WILLOW
AND THE
BRIDGE

Poems and Meditations
by Toyohiko Kagawa
and
Franklin Cole

ASSOCIATION PRESS — NEW YORK — 1947

137

Dedication

To Him who unites us
In spite of oceans that divide us;
To Him — stronger, deeper, purer than oceans —
Our Lord, our Saviour, our Hope.

About the Authors

Seldom have two persons so dissimilar in experience, age, reputation, national background, and outlook joined in publishing a volume of their writings. "Our differences, however, are small," they contend, "compared with our unity and brotherhood in the Christian faith."

Toyohiko Kagaka has long been world-famous for his saintly character, his reforming zeal, his literary talents, his Christian witness in word and deed. He has been called 'the Japanese St. Francis,' which rightly describes his humility and Christian devotion but does not compass his many pioneering activities in the fields of education, economics, social organization, and religion. Among the institutions he has launched and supported in Japan are united Protestant churches, rural and industrial co-operatives, kindergartens for the children of working mothers, a research bureau for farmers and laborers, several periodicals, an ex-prisoners' home, an employment agency for girls, a number of settlement houses of which six, in Kobe, Osaka, and Tokyo, were burned in B29 raids. Christians of the world have looked to him for an unfailing witness, as did Mme. Chiang Kai-shek in the darkest days of the war in China: "I can pray for the Japanese people," she wrote, "knowing that there must be many, like Kagawa, who suffer because of what their country is doing."

Kagawa's grief and persecution (including three arrests and one imprisonment in solitary confinement) during the war-years have triumphantly ended. He is now giving himself unstintingly to Christian preaching and education, an evangelistic campaign of "three million lives for Christ in three years," relief work among his suffering people (for whom he received large grants of lumber and rice from the Allied authorities after Japanese government officials had failed), leadership in organizing various groups into a Social Democratic Party of Japan, and the task of developing and leading his "International Peace Association," which he founded at the suggestion of the Premier. He who was driven underground during the war-years has arisen again into the stature of his greatest reputation and influence, at least among his own people. *Asahi*, having the largest circulation of all Tokyo newspapers, recently acclaimed him as "the Apostle of Liberation." For the economic, political, and spiritual liberation of his fellow countrymen from their tragic bondage of the past, Dr. Kagawa is giving his full strength and devotion. He had planned to write a new peace poem for this volume, but he confessed to his associate, "I wrote a few lines and tore up the page. I'm so tired at the end of each day that my thoughts won't 'jell' into poetry."

Franklin Cole is a native of rural Indiana. He was educated at DePauw, Boston, and Oxford Universities, and has traveled through Europe, the Mediterranean countries, and the Orient. He has served as minister of Williston Church, Portland, Maine, and the Church-in-the-Gardens, Forest Hills, New York, and as radio minister with the Federal Council of Churches of Christ in America. During the war he served as chaplain in the United States Naval Reserve. He was aboard one of the ships of the Advance Task Force of Halsey's Third Fleet which entered Tokyo Bay on August 28, 1945. He spent the first night in Tokyo Bay writing the sonnet, "To Kagawa." A few days later he was the first American chaplain to visit Kagawa. During his three months in Japan, Chaplain Cole regularly visited the Japanese Christians, provided them with hundreds of New Testaments, and rendered other material and spiritual assistance. He has returned to his New York pastorate and radio ministry. During the summer in Maine, he directs Camp Kagawa, an interracial camp of Japanese, Chinese, Negro, and white boys from New York City.

As Kagawa and Cole stated in their agreement, signed and witnessed in Tokyo, "This joint-work is undertaken by the authors in the spirit of Christian witness, which we believe must span every barrier of nation and race."

1947   THE EDITORS

The Authors' Preface

The purpose of this slender volume, it should be evident, is not to pit literary style against style, nationality against nationality, nor the experience of one author against that of the other. Our differences of background and outlook, while they have not been consciously minimized by either of us, are small indeed compared with the spiritual unity and brotherhood we share in the Christian faith. In sorrow and humility we have seen the grief and suffering caused by sin, and the separation of man from man, nation from nation, class from class. We hope that by our co-operative labors we have helped to construct one small section of the bridge that will someday unite our peoples again in an understanding and brotherly spirit.

And I heard a great voice out of heaven saying, Behold, the tabernacle of God is with man, and he will dwell with them, and they shall be his people, and God himself shall be with them and be their God.

And God shall wipe away all tears from their eyes; and there shall be no more death, neither sorrow, nor crying, neither shall there be any more pain. . . . Behold I make all things new.

TOYOHIKO KAGAWA
FRANKLIN COLE

1947

Contents

Meditations by Toyohiko Kagawa

(Freely edited by his permission and given personalized settings
by Franklin Cole)

The Willow and the Bridge

A willow, head bent low,
And weeping gentle tears into a pool;

Beyond the pool, unyielding bridge
Of ancient, tested rocks;

A picture in Japan
And of Japan.

The people bow like willows,
Weep o'er sins that cursed the past,

And sorrows now—too deep
Almost for weeping.

The bridge beyond, is standing still,
A landmark of the centuries.

The common folk, bowed by their grief,
Shall yet arise with freedom, vision, strength,

To cross the bridge, to leave the pool,
And set their faces toward the mounts
Whose summits beckon with the hand
Of clear, cold Dawn.

FRANKLIN COLE

Poems by
TOYOHIKO KAGAWA

The Willow

Ah tears! Unbidden tears!
Familiar friends in childhood's lonely years:
Long separated we.
Why do you come again to dwell with me?
With deepest sorrow and unyielding scorn,
You mirror China by my brothers torn—
Your witness I accept.
But I'm no coward; pray heed e'er more you've wept:
I love Japan so fair,
And China too; this war I cannot bear.

'Is there no other way'?
Thus do I search my spirit all the day,
Nor yet attain the answer's goal.
I live, but as a contrite soul.
Like Christ who bore our sins upon the Cross,
I too must bear my country's sin and dross.
Land of my love, thy sins are grievous to be borne;
My head is bowed upon this form forlorn.
Ah tears! Unbidden tears! Long separated we!
But now, as in my childhood years,
My soul is washed by flowing tears.

The Flame of the Holy Ghost

O, the heart that is bleeding,
The blood that is boiling,
Awaiting the answer to prayer.
Blaze up, flame of Holy Ghost!
Blaze up, and scorch the sky!

O fire of the Cross,
Blaze up in North America!
Run over the continent;
Pour out the molten Word
Of the Cross!

The blood of me,
A son of man,
Has dried up.

What to do?
Wait . . .
Wait for the flame of Holy Ghost!

Prayer All Through the Night

Around a brazier,
And on the cold earth
We kneel.
We pray for peace.
The Pacific (named wisely by man)
Must still be pacific, God willing.

The darkness deepens,
Yet our prayer goes deeper than darkness;
Our prayer goes on forever!

On the other shores of this Ocean,
Our friends, our brothers in prayer,
Must also be grieving and waiting,
Waiting for Dawn to come.

Our prayers have not been answered
These ten, long, heavy, tragic years!
We shall bear the lid
Of the coffin on our backs . . .
And pray.

Via Dolorosa

With sorrowful heart,
Yet for the joy of atonement,
You went, O Christ, to Calvary.

If the stars ceased to twinkle
And the sun forgot to shine,
The ever-increasing rays of God's love
Would find an earthward passage
Through you.

O Christ,
That a thousand and a thousand years
Have passed since Golgotha you braved;
And still men gasp with fear
And grasp with greed—and suffer:
Let us swing into the orbit of your love.

Hasten the day
When we can forget the borders of countries,
The hues of the skin;
When we—all of us together—
Can praise in harmony your love.

O, let us see more vividly
Your blood of love from Calvary,
Streaming like ever-increasing rays . . .
Earthward.

Death Is My Art

Death is my art,
Like the art of Light.
She glows; she guides us all.
On selfless shafts
She gives her all—
Gives her life to others,
And flees away.

Like Light, I give my life
To others—may they live!
I die for Emperor and people.
I am caught in the cosmic embrace;
In it I give my all, forgive man's all,
And nestle close to God.

I shed my blood here, everywhere,
Like drops of universal light,
Like Christ, high lifted-up
On Calvary.

Better Believe in Miracles

What miracles would be in store
For men who deserted this world—
For men who started from zero.

They would see life anew,
Like the sun on each venturesome round.
All darkness confound
With the innocency of dawn.

To them sharp agony
Or high tragedy
Would become a miracle of nothingness—
Like snow hiding scars on Fuji-san's brow.

But there are miracles greater than nothing,
Far greater than zero.
You know them; better believe in them.
Believe strongly!

Poem Without Words

When nothing happens,
When I'm without trouble,
(Though conscious of many troubles,)
I keep a silence with Heaven
And breathe with face upward
Like a tree-top.

Heaven speaks without speaking;
Nature speaks—and with silence;
The embryo grows but it speaks not,
Knows not how to speak, but it grows.
Christ, through Pilate's confusion, is silent
As on to the Cross he goes.

Stars speak not—still they witness;
Flowers sing not—yes, they do!
Color and light have voice
More than voice
And song more than song.

These, I think, are gospels of the Rhythmic Silence—
Poems without words.

When I Sit in Darkness

When I sit in the darkness of meditation,
Even the darkness and coldness of prison,
Quietly . . .
My life communicates with God.
He whispers within when other forms
Of communication are lost.
I see him within
When outerness is darkness.

Creator, create anew love within me.
Broken am I; begin thy repairing.
The triumph is this:
God, through my consciousness,
Begins a new world-reformation.

God Who Feeds Even the Fly

When I was locked up in the cell
Of the 'thought-control' Kempeitai prison,
I was taught a lesson by a fly.
(Insect life was present there!)

It has no horns or teeth;
Devoid of scales and hooves and poison;
It has no armies, navies, or planes:
Yet it lives—
A pacifistic, persistent little creature!

God, who feeds even the fly,
Will also care for me—
A worthless being like me.

I Am a Child of the Sun

I am a child of the Sun,
And a son of Japan:

The Sea is my mother,
  The Sun is paternal,
The Cherry my nurse,
  And Fuji fraternal.

Everything under the sun
  Is my bed;
All the bright stars
  Jewel the hood of my head.

The rims of volcanoes—
  My glittering rings;
And trees form the notes
  On my robe as it sings.

I am a child of the soil—
  Yellow skin testifies;
But of spirit and soul,
  A son of the skies!

Walking in the Sky

The rumor of war,
The hatred of propaganda,
Reach out their blackened fingers
Toward me; I have already
Escaped them. My heart is in heaven!

On earth I wander
And am never lonesome.
The world of destiny,
Though often barricaded,
Is never narrow.

I walk with Heaven every day—
A day in the sky.
Today again, as yesterday,
I shall walk in the sky
With the sun.

All Are Adornments for My Soul

When being misunderstood,
I stand quietly.
When accused,
I bear bravely.

Though poor,
I try to make many rich.
Having little to cover my bones,
I have everything for my heart.

Grief is not grief
And pain not pain to me now.
Through life and death, in prayer
I go back to my Father's love.

Even earth offers, like jewels,
Her recompensing glories:
The hedges, brooks, ponds, and farming villages—
All are adornments for my soul!

Invention Is a Gift from Heaven

1. High above the fleecy clouds,
      Mount Fuji stands and sings;
   The rising sun above the mount
      Scatters scent of early spring.

   (Refrain)
      The power of invention boils
         In the furnace and its blaze.
      Invention is a holy gift,
         Like the Heaven's rays!

2. The heat of August, molten iron,
      Shall never weaken toil.
   To melt the darkness of the East
      Young blood was meant to boil.

3. Unlike our globe-flower, only blooms,
      That brings no fruit to sight,
   Our furnace, lo! it bears the fruit
      Of toiling Love and Light.

4. Out of the darkness of the world,
      The light shall dawn, we pray;
   Let's pioneer to help mankind,
      Pursue the glory-path this day.

   (Refrain)
      The power of invention boils
         In the furnace and its blaze.
      Invention is a holy gift,
         Like the Heaven's rays!

The Day of Completion

With pangs many,
Through struggle severe,
You were born.
They die as you live.

Grow up, babe,
Without fear!
They who cursed your birth
Shall beg to adopt you.

O child of miracle!
As led by God, (you shall be!)
Surging waves will calm at eve,
A friendly cloud will lead your way
By day.

O, the Okinawas, Children of the Ocean

The ocean gave birth to the Okinawas,
And to the eagles of mountain-high nests,
And to sea-faring boys who return to motherly arms.

'Climbing out on a branch,
Climbing out on seven branches—
Laying one egg,
Laying seven eggs!
Out of this one egg,
Out of the seven,
The eagle of beautiful wings was born.
On New Year's Day he flew from the nest,
In early morning of New Year's Day;
He flew away toward the East,
Dancing on ripples of sky toward the Sun.'

(Yaeyama sings: so strange, so wistfully!)

Ah, the boys of Okinawa who fly toward the Sun
Are the children born of the ocean.
Sea-tide, kiss thy sons of courage!
They fear not the raging wave,
The typhoon they calmly brave
On the two-hundred-tenth day.

O, the land of my mother, Okinawa!
So exhausted now thy people,
Poor, downtrodden, and exploited.
But here is one, at least, who sings a song,
Praying the eagle's return.
Ah, Okinawa, dear Okinawa!
I will sing a new song for you—
Mother of my mother,
Child of the ocean.

Let the sun evaporate your tears!

33

Tsuzumi, a Hand Drum

Purely and clearly
The sound of tsuzumi is heard.
Breaking through twilight,
Piercing through pain
Like a thrusting sword,
The sound of the hand-drum
Stabs my awareness.

In China, India,
Lands of the West—
Never a sound like this!
It urges me to forget and bury
All earthly sense:
Fear, attachment, resentment.
The evening hand-drum
Beats on my heart.

As our souls march on
Piercing the world-darkness,
Strike the tsuzumi!
Sound out the soul of Yamato,
Cleanse out the evil from earth,
And lead us toward realms of the Pure!

Musaski Plain Shall Remember

Tokutomi Kenjiro—child of Nature,
Charmed by potential leaves in the springtime,
Mind with the rhythm of reeds on Musashi,
Soul brimmed with lava from Fuji-san's cup!
So Kenjiro, fed by the soil and the seasons,
Grew strong, innocent, trustful—like Adam.

He preached true love for the Highest.
Among the camellias, the oaks, and the chestnuts,
(Even the briars and thorns of the roadside),
He lived the Kingdom of Heaven,
He plumbed to the depths of atonement.
The soul of Japan was he.

Autumn returns to Musashi again:
The miscanthus plumes forth like a princess;
The chestnuts ripen with gold.
And again, with memorial beauty,
The Plain of Musashi remembers
Tokutomi Kenjiro,
And praises God's name.

Defender of soul and things lovely,
Can you sleep in peace, Rokwa Tokutomi,
While the earth quakes with war and its rumors?
Do your dreams throb not with our troubles?
Peace—yes, the peace that you sought to anchor
Is slipping away—like a tossed ship from moorings.

So when the miscanthus puts forth plumes again,
Come in our midst and fight for us then.
Japan, like Musashi, can never forget you.
Arise, come, strive for the peace of the world!
Tokutomi Kenjiro, son of the Highest!

Poems by
FRANKLIN COLE

To Kagawa

Thou Flower of Christ, whose petalled goodness swept
    Across a world too barren to behold or to receive;
Whose reconciling word of love too deep, too deft,
    For sworded men to fathom or believe:
I come to this, your isle, with poignant sight
    Of rubbled ashes where a city ought to be;
Forgive me that I come encloaked in naval might,
    When that my only weapon were a calloused knee!
To you I come to offer not my terms,
    But to receive the Christlike terms you know;
And with you on your mercied turns
    Among your burdened brothers I would go.
Ah grief, that you, no stranger to Cross-bearing,
Cannot hear us and use us, who hunger for Cross-sharing!

I Removed My Shoes

I removed my shoes—
And stepped into a home.

There I found
Faith's *tokonoma;*
A scroll of simple beauty
With canary on a bamboo twig;
Three flowers that harmonized and sang
Of Earth and Man and Heaven;
The sunlit tea of friendship,
Blessing and uniting
Two men of East and West.

I'm glad that I removed my shoes.

The Dispossessed

No eye can see them all;
No heart can feel
The throbbing anguish of their fate—
Perhaps a fool to try.

They lived their lives upon an earth
That rumbled; nothing sound or solid;
Then the inevitable! The rumble
Became a blast. The lid
Of trembling rocks blew up,
And up in shattered bits
Went homes and heirlooms—everything—
Everything but people.
They were caught by the lava of war.
The countless dead from the burning!
The millions and millions of people,
Breath of our breath and touch of our touch,
Still caught in the throes of the lava.
The fight to be free, to bandage the wounds,
To build life anew—no end to all this
In our span of time.

O God, dispossess me
Of all that would wither my clasp
Of hand and heart with the folk dispossessed.
If my home—burn it!
If my acre of land—scorch it
Of greenness and harvest!
If my slender purse—rob me!
No chains must hold me from oneness
With the dispossessed.

If on You let me live
With few possessions, hyssop my soul!
Acid out my indifference
Till it gurgles with fury!
From anguish the balm of compassion.
Ignite my prejudice, burn it to cinders;
And from the ashes let rise
The shrines of mercy and radiant faith.
Dispossess my heart of its evils
And I shall possess Man, Heaven, and You.

Where Is Thy God?

It's a terrible thought that God is in this war—
That a Pilgrim from the cosmic silence should be caught
    in deafening fray;
That the Law-giver should see his laws, graven on ancient
    slabs,
Carried by lawless men—back, back, beyond the shades
    of Sinai;
That the Lifegiver, who gave man breath for his nostrils,
Length and breadth to his years, should stand between
    the furrows
Of a fallen flesh: "These men I gave to have dominion!"

It is a terrible thought that God is in this war;
More awful still the thought that he is not.
Could God — and still be God — remain aloof in astral
    silence,
While agonizing man is piercing heaven with his cries?
Could God, Law-giver and the Judge, turn blinded eye
Upon the wrongs of men and nations' infamy?
Would tares be sown another spring if, by an alchemy
    divine,
This harvest turned to wheat?

God is in this war—a Pilgrim from the silence in the fray;
A giver of the Law which mocked shall never be;
A Giver of the Life, who yet upon a Cross,
Shall be released, redeemed, and lifted up,
Up to magnetic power and universal sovereignty.

43

Who Shall Remember?

Who shall remember
This quaking day of imperial history,
When rocks of tradition, ambition, and conquest
Are shaken (and shattered maybe) to unplumbable
    depths?
These swords and medals, these pens, this parchment—
Who shall remember?

The sun will not remember, for he saw not,
And never in a spiteful mood be tempted
To break a hurtful secret to the goddess Amaterasu.
The clouds, high-ceilinged, may have seen;
And if perchance they saw, they'll soon forget,
Come rain at evening or tomorrow's dawn.

Mount Fuji too is spared the sight,
As though he ordered slaves of mist and fog
To stretch a heavy veil before his wearied eyes.
No lesser hill, no site of town or plain
Can e'er lock up the scene to brood in anguish
Till a psychopathic chieftain hears the groan:
'Avenge this site! Death is a feather!' . . . and obeys.
The sun is not a witness nor a rock of sacred land:
Who shall remember?

Oh yes, this deck of super-warship
Where the signers meet—it shall remember
For a season, (though decks can rust, and at their best
Leave imprints few to cherish or to talk about).

Who shall remember? These:
The little, rippling waves upon this wind-stirred bay—

44

They shall remember. Lapping this gaunt prow
They seem to catch the word and feel the import
Of this hour. Now they scurry on, whispering,
Whispering each to her neighbor, till Tokyo Wan
Is rippling with feminine whispers no censor can hush.
So on to the shore, increasing in numbers and boldness,
As others speed outward beyond Yokosuka,
Beyond the last gateway that guards Tateyama.
Anon the coy waves, rippling still with their secrets,
Are caught in masculine arms, protective, possessive.

Carry the word, ye earth-circling billows,
The word of recompense, freedom, and justice:
Chains for the tyrants, mercy for innocents,
The word of law, understanding, and friendship!
Carry the word, and shout it to rocks and the sands
Of every atoll, island, and mainland
Where the man-creatures dwell. Stir them,
You billows of witness, with dreadnaught dreams
Of a world that's round, that's organic of body,
And must be of spirit and mind united and peaceful.
Pound home the lesson; uplift the low vision!
Capture the souls of men for out-charted horizons . . .
And they shall remember.

The Last Time Over Tokyo

The last time over Tokyo we flew,
At end of autumn's peaceful day,
The setting sun was like a harvest moon,
And stars were not of heaven but of earth:
Bits of shattered glass, like jewels in rubbled heaps,
Mirrored up the rays and twinkled at the plane.
And there below—a man of burden bowed,
Searching, sifting, scattering the debris:
Broken glass to him—a levelled home—not stars.

O God, could I but take that weary brother,
Lift him to these heights and show him
Stars of witness, stars of promise—whatever they may be.
Or better still, could I but wing to earth
A potent thing of science that in a magic moment
Would rebuild those twisted ruins, rebuild the homes
Our man-made terrors once destroyed!
The pathos that I have but prayers to give:
Prayers of anguish, sadness, and repentance,
Prayers for peace and faith and understanding;
Such as they are, O Lord, they're mirrored up,
Shining fragments of a war-torn soul.

The Hedgerows of God

I remember the hedgerows of God
That bordered the ploughed Hoosier field,
The hedgerows of elder and briar,
Where the violets played hide-and-go-seek
With the breeze and the coy April sun;
Where the guinea hen mothered her young;
Where the flora was wild, and the song
Of the thrush and the sparrow rolled forth,
Not as duet, but fully in tune
With the natural wildness.
Those singing, unkempt hedgerows of God!

Now I'm hemmed in by the hedgerows of man
That border this gundeck.
So precise are the hedgerows—mathematical, deadly,
That birds would not nest here,
No rabbit would rest here; only man
Is doomed to watch and to wait.
No music this hedgerow; its discordant prose
Is but the staccato of engines gone mad.
Wildness is here, but the wildness of death-throes;
Singing I hear—from hell's guttural throats.
These stark, steel, cacophonous hedgerows of man!

O, to return to the wild Hoosier hedgerows!
Return, O Man, to the hedgerows of God!

The Anchoring Pull

The time has come and the place is here—
As good as any to drop the hook
Into the purplish blue and see the gurgle,
Then feel the shudder, tug, and tension,
The anchoring pull to a restless ship.
I mean to say, (O God, the wit to say it better!)
That now on deeps and islets of Oceania—
Alien to the prairie farm near Pierceton,
Where corn's in tassel, orchards bright with cherries—
On death-defying, death-inviting missions,
That too are foreign to my training
Of 'plant and reap and gather into barns';
Now, now, if ever, I must riddle out the riddle,
Or failing that, set down a thing or two.

This endless ploughing 'twixt Polaris and the Southern
     Cross,
(With ne'er a lasting furrow to give the proof of it;)
This global war that shrinks to the provincial:
The state of this our ship, our chow, our gunpower;
This lofty talk of 'freedoms' and of 'charters',
While youth is herded into holds unfit for cattle,
Disgorged on this dead atoll, that dread beach-head.
(The market's up two points; peace rumors groundless!)
With moods as changing as this Ocean monster,
Wild and winsome, smiling and typhoon-infested,
So must I write. So must I write
To keep the knack of writing through sterile months
That eye no art with favor; to paint a few impressions
That stand out—distant palm groves through the dawn.
But this o'er all, to seek the truth that's tideless,
To find a faith that arches heaven to earth,
And heart to heart and God to man.

48

No Poppies Here

No poppies here, for row on row
    The crosses rise from whitened coral;
It is no friend of things that grow
    Like flower and shrub—and that's the moral:

The coral takes of rain and light,
    Transforms them not to floral reds,
But blesses with angelic white:
    White crosses *bloom* in coral beds.

This evening, then, if sound were sight,
    The threnody of rain would pave
With tear-buds, wreathed in Easter white,
    The coral and cross of many a grave.

These Ways of Air, These Lanes of Sea

These ways of air, these lanes of sea,
    Were charted not in Cosmic plan;
Within God's fluid air and sea
    The routes were carved by will of man.

And man? He held the globe of God,
    Drew fiery lines through air and sea.
The fire stayed not within the lanes:
    It threatens global destiny.

Why So Class-conscious?

Fire-bomb,
American fire-bomb,
Why so class-conscious?
Why did you come to the poor—
The poor of the slums and the valleys,
And give them your warming embrace?

You insulted the rich and the powerful,
The barons who live on the hilltops,
The court- and mart-princes of seashores;
Too busy to visit them? Too merciful
Lavishing gifts, like an angel of Christmas,
On hearthstones of hovels?

Fire-bomb,
Saintly fire-bomb,
Friend of the poor!

That was Hiroshima—once prolific town
Where paper parasols of rainbow hues
Were born and first tried out their wings.
Schools were there: Buddhist, public, Methodist;
And gabled temples climbed into the skies.
What of chimneys venting smoke of war,
And ships with martial cargo sailing out?
Homes and fruit trees, shrines and brothels,
The good and bad of every city;
People, young and old, slave and master,
People mostly poor—three times a hundred thousand of
    them—
All were there in what was Hiroshima.

This the Hiroshima that we saw:
A flattened hand that had been scorched,
Extending its gaunt fingers through the tidal bay
As though to balm away the pain.
The veins within the hand that were canals,
The seared hairs of the hand that once were trees,
The broken warts that were the concrete frames
Of banks; the ashen flesh that once was living homes.
In all, a hand fired to the quick.

What shall it be—this thing called Hiroshima?
The ash of science that was once the flame?
The tempting fruit that long had been forbidden?
The obelisk to man, his pride and prowess,
Who split a little world and lost a sovereign soul?
Or shall it be—this thing called Hiroshima—
The curtain falling on an ancient globe
That went careening through the chartless space,

Stopped at the brink of hell? The curtain rising
On a world, sparkling new as April morn,
And blessed with promise for enduring peace?
What shall it be—the shroud of passing man
Or cradle of rebirth? The choice is ours.

Christ's world or none since Hiroshima:
The choice is stark as that!
Time there was, unfolding wave on wave,
When man could swim between alternatives—
Light and outer darkness, peace and total war.
But violent undertow has gripped the sea of time,
And man, the swimmer, fights for limb and life.
What hand can save if not the Hand of Christ?

Since Hiroshima . . . what?

Meditations by

TOYOHIKO KAGAWA

(Freely edited by his permission and given personalized
settings by Franklin Cole)

Blessed Poverty

A certain rich man said to the Poor Man: "You have ability, originality, and a world-wide following. May I ask why you are not wealthy?" And the Poor Man said:

Once I had a little money, but, shamed by the sight of so many people who have nothing, I scattered it away.

Thus I am always pursued by the wolf of poverty.

But do not pity me. It is easier to be poor than to worry about possessions. As long as God gives me strength to keep one step ahead of the wolf, I am content.

In the stress of fleeing the blood-thirsty pursuer, I am conscious of God's presence, and that is indeed blessed.

More often poverty to me is a lamb—innocent, pure, and Christ-like. In green pastures and beside still waters, I lie down in peace with the holy lamb.

Non-possession of things is a blessing for which I thank God.

To have nothing does not mean inability to possess. It means non-possession in spite of the power to possess.

One does not need to become a beggar like St. Francis in order to be religious. Both St. Francis and Buddha erred in glorifying the beggar. Better to work, earn, and give away than not to work, and to beg, and to receive from those who have worked, earned, and given away.

To possess nothing does not mean that one has no desire to possess. The will to non-possession grows through the continuing struggle to become like God—God, Mind and Spirit, free even of the material world He created.

Blessed poverty! Sometimes like a wolf; sometimes like a lamb; and again like God!

Rich Paupers: Poor Millionaires

On a later occasion when they met, the Poor Man taught the rich man in a less philosophical, more homely and illustrative vein:

Some people are rich paupers. Though they possess a million yen, they want more and more—more houses, more servants, more automobiles, more amusements. I call them rich paupers.

But there are others who are rich in poverty. They have either mastered their selfish desires or have learned to live abundantly on what they have. They are the truly rich.

The poor in the slums are happier than others because they share even their poverty. But the rich who yearn to be richer cannot share even a yen of their wealth without pain.

If you try to increase your possessions, you are always in a turmoil.

When you have a book, you want a book-case; then you need a room for the book-case; then a house to shelter the room; then land for the house; and at last a whole country for your estate.

The spiral grows like a typhoon and finally sucks in the man who blew only a breath of covetousness.

There is nothing more bothersome than to try to live in affluence.

When the wind blows, you worry about the garden; when it rains you worry about the roof. The more gardens and roofs you have, the more your worries are multiplied.

Since I love simplicity and hate bother, I never crave modern life. I want to remain a son of Nature.

Blessed be poverty; happy is he who is rich therein.

Christ's Fool

"I am looking for wisdom," said a student after morning chapel, as he and the Preacher walked along the maple-studded college path. "You are a wise man, sir, and I would know your secret of wisdom." And the Preacher answered:

No, not wise in any worldly sense. I could be wise, perhaps, if that were my desire—even as I could have money if I wished to cling to it. But neither wisdom nor money is mine.

You see, I am a fool—a fool for Christ. I do not boast of it, for I have no other choice.

Before the age of fifteen, I prayed *with my head under the covers:* O God, make me like Christ. But in my fifteenth year, I pledged myself and Him that no one else would ever usurp my love for Him, and to this day my pledge has been kept.

Ask me what has been the passion of my days; I cannot answer, Woman, but must answer, Christ. For his sake I restrain human love, and for his sake I forsake many natural, sinful inclinations.

I am his captive, his slave, his fool.

And I walk not the glittering broadway of learning, arts, discoveries, and inventions. I walk the humble, hillside path that may lead to one lost sheep.

Love, the Law of Life

A man of science challenged, "The law of life is natural selection; the life-medium is selfishness, and the iron-clad fact of life is 'the survival of the fittest.'" To which the Man of Love replied:

By those standards, you doubtless would have been born and would have grown to maturity. But not I who lack both selfishness and fitness. Nature made an error when she "selected" me!

I hold that selfishness is self-defeating unless the ego is lost in the common good. Unless man gives and receives sustenance from the whole tree of life, he becomes a severed twig and withers away.

Aborigines can still be found who practice cannibalism. Some of them are strong physical specimens. But they are a dying race. They exhaust themselves in fighting and killing. They are so non-cooperative that they cannot even build a house by united efforts. So they have no houses or schools or churches. They have no art of life, and they are losing the struggle for life.

Truly, love is the law of life. But let me explain what I mean by love. It has three stages.

First, there is instinctive love like that of parents for children, husbands for wives, even apes for apes. Instinctive love is the root, but not the flower of life.

Second, there is "the semi-conscious" stage of love. A nurse may serve her patients, however infectious or loathsome their diseases. But there is a limit to this kind of love. The same nurse, when she meets an enemy who has said cruel or false things about her, may not be able to forgive and love that enemy.

The highest stage is fully conscious love. Jesus could

love sinners and even his enemies. Why? Because his consciousness was above the average human level—above instinctive love, above semi-conscious love. His consciousness was of God.

One cannot discover the law of life if one fails to reckon with the Creator and Redeemer of life. As well try to discover the secret of this blade of grass without taking into account its seed, earth, and sunshine!

Love is the final word, for God is love. Whoever fails to learn this truth or receive this power is like an electric bulb which has been divorced from the dynamo.

This is the gospel: "Whosoever loveth not, knoweth not God, for God is love."

To know not God is to have no law of life—and worse. To know not God is to be dead to life.

God is life! God is love!

Love, Truth, and Growth

A child, large of mind for his slender years, said, "I want to grow in truth. How shall I do it?" The Loving Teacher said:

You are right in wanting to grow in truth; you might say *into* truth.

It is you who grows. Truth has the possibility of growth, but it does not grow of and by itself. It grows with and through you as you penetrate and understand some of its mysteries.

With new experience comes new truth. Man grows eternally—and thus encourages the seed of truth to grow.

If truth be a seed, love is the fertilizer to encourage its growth. Love is more—it is the essence of the universe. To me, love is the *Ding an Sich* (reality) of Kant.

The true essence of the ever-growing universe is maternal love, expressing itself in the process of growth.

When love is new and powerful in man, truth grows in the world. There is no miracle like love. Love is the miracle worker.

Child, if you would grow in truth, grow first in love. Grow, that truth and love through you may grow!

Like Man, Like Nature

An amateur painter of landscapes said to the Man of Nature: "I have the gift of putting on canvas what I see in nature. But somehow the paintings do not glow with life—they are precise and dead as a geometrical design. What to do?" The Man of Nature said:

Do you not paint your thoughts and dreams into your landscapes? Only they can make your paintings live. Mix bright pigments with your soul and not your fingers!

All nature is not beautiful. Nature wears a silken bridal gown or patched-up rags, depending on the sight of those who approach her.

Brilliant sunshine is cursed by the sorrowful heart, but the foul water in a slum-gutter is like a bubbling spring to a happy, loving soul.

If you listen not with your open heart, nature speaks not with her open heart. To the innocent soul, the stream of the mountain flows with God.

To medieval men, who lived in fear and anxiety, nature was a nest of evil spirits. But to modern man who loves and understands nature, the nest is filled with song.

Only those who dwell in the bosom of God take nature to their own bosoms.

The poet communes with the field-lilies because he loves them. Responsively, sometimes in unison, they read the litany of love together.

Before the advent of great love, nature was unfathomable.

True nature-lovers are they who love the soul, and find the soul in nature as in man.

Suffering Is an Art

People came to him during a certain one of his illnesses, one of many, and sought to condole him saying, "You must be bored with your long illness, when your work is waiting." To certain of his callers, but more often to himself, the Sufferer said:

I know there is work waiting for me, but I live not for work; I live for life.

If I think of tomorrow's task, I may miss this moment and forfeit the peace of many hours today.

My life is *now*. The goal of every minute, even on this sick bed, is to be with God. So I do not think of tomorrow or the day after tomorrow. I do not even think of the hours after sunset today.

Always thankful to God that I live happily with Him every moment, I am conscious of no boredom.

Suffering is an art—the highest of all arts. Only Almighty God and they who are in his tender care can enjoy this art.

Only they who believe that God creates suffering can accept it as an art.

The fine arts of God are sown in suffering and reaped in life.

He who dwells constantly upon his own suffering has not learned how to conquer. But he who bears suffering for the sake of God makes of suffering an art.

Herein lies the significance of the Cross. To us the Cross is sad and cruel and repulsive, but to the carpenter, Jesus, it was the glory of ecstasy and fulfillment. In the sanctification of Christ's suffering lives the ultimate art of God.

Behold suffering, the highest art!

If one can conquer suffering, one can also conquer joy and success.

To him who can overcome the sorrows and ills of the world, can there remain any evil?

Strife Makes Void

"How shall we think of strife?" asked a disciple who was wavering between idealistic pacifism and realistic preparedness. The Man of Peace answered:

Strife makes void all inner life.

Do not ask me to explain this, for it is the source of my deepest sorrow.

Through strife Babylon, Greece, and Rome perished. On the same bloody road the modern nations pour forth their life and resources.

Science does not exterminate humanity; rather it is strife which destroys mankind. Science produces bigger and more deadly tools, but they wield not themselves. Only in vicious hands do the tools become vicious.

For the natural adjustment of the power to conquer, man mechanizes everything. Races of people are hardened by militarism.

The bud of inventive genius is blighted by the torrid winds of strife.

Ask a horticultural genius where evolution occurs in the wild violet—on a bleak hillside or in a warm hothouse. The wild violet on the hillside wastes its energy in strife against an unfriendly environment—the energy that might have been used in evolution if it were given a constant, peaceful environment.

In order to evolve, organic energy must be used for a definite purpose. But when the energy is misused in strife, the evolving function ceases.

So a long era of peace is necessary if man would build a high culture.

Violence and Non-Resistance

The Man of Peace continued to hold forth the pearls of wisdom which, growing in wounds of his soul, he had suffered and struggled to bring to their mature beauty:

Non-resistance does not mean cowardice; rather it means restraint from inflicting harm on others.

Non-resistance calls for teamwork of ideals, not timidity of instincts.

Some persons think it means no resistance to evil. But that is error. Evil must be resisted, but not with evil.

Evil against evil inflicts death—not to the evil but to the good.

Evil and evil struggling together are locked, not in throes of destruction, but in the act of propagation. Evil against evil produces a devilish offspring.

"Can Satan cast out Satan?"

Only love can resist and conquer evil, as only God can resist and conquer Satan.

Love eternally progresses, counting not the cost.

A loving person is willing to be murdered, but not to murder others.

One who fears the sacrifice of love must resort to violence, but one who believes in sacrificial love practices non-violence.

Herein lies personal and social evolution. To him who is forever growing and evolving, there is an eternal Cross.

For the creation of the co-operative society, love is indispensable.

Love is plus.

Violence is minus.

Violence is suicidal.

Love is progressive, reproductive, and eternal.

On Making Common Things Holy

A common man said to the Uncommon Man, "Speak to us of common things and holy things"; to which he replied:

All things of earth and stars are common—and all can be holy.

There is a vast difference between making holiness commonplace and making the commonplace holy.

To drink deeply from God's cup, and to find mystery hidden in the common tasks and duties of daily life, are indeed blessed.

But to refuse that sacrament in order to practice the alchemy of turning sacredness into commonness is sin.

To take God's grace for granted is to fall from His grace.

The degeneration of religion accompanies the mechanization of the holy life.

He errs who makes the function of his flesh a god; but he who thinks of his body as the temple of God enters into the true knowledge of the glory of the flesh.

I await the day when holiness will control the commonplace, but I rejoice not as I see holiness enslaved by the common, vulgar, ruthless forces of our day.

The common man becomes a saint, not by any act of external canonization. He is a saint who has the inner vision of seeing God in all common things, and the inner power of transforming the secular into the sacred.

An uncommon diamond is common carbon that has been crystallized into the beauty of holiness.

Life Shadowed with Tears

When he was asked, "How can one best make use of adversity?" the Man of Tears said:

If you concentrate on what you have, rather than on what you never have had or have lost, you shall be happy.

If I lose one eye and have only dim sight in the other, I still have sight. Even if I lose both eyes and my ears remain, the outer world of truth and music will enter my soul on auditory wings. Or if the natural functions of eyes and ears fail me, and my nose remains—as long as something of sense remains—my life is richer than if I had nothing.

With such an outlook, I congratulate myself on my good fortune, even though I experience great sorrow.

Once I wished to die and leave this troublesome world. But not now! As I dwelt on the calmness of the future life, this life became increasingly dramatic and interesting. After all, life shadowed with tears is better than a flat, drab, ever-sunny existence.

Have I told you of my palace of jewels? I saw it as I gazed from my sick bed.

The sunlight, reflected on the window pane, grew into a palace. And the lines on the palm of my hand became avenues of sapphire that led me to the palace.

I saw it all through tears!

The Eternal Woman

A woman came to the Man, who was not a monk or a bachelor, but a happily married husband and father, to hear his thoughts on womanhood. He who has given great leadership to the cause of raising the social status of women in the Orient, said:

Woman can tell man of the mystery of life, for she is destined to think deeply about it.

It is her calling to think about and perform the three functions of life which are no doubt life's greatest: pregnancy, birth, and the rearing of children.

As a mother, she is conscious of her responsibility to rear her children in the way of truth and purity, which can best be done by the help of God.

It is noteworthy that throughout the world, women are religious-minded. In the churches of the West, women compose two-thirds of the congregations.

She is more religious than man—not because she is weaker or more sentimental, but because she is more intimately concerned and occupied with the mysteries of life.

On the summits of experience, as in the valley of the shadow, she is high priestess of those mysteries.

Her faith exalts her and gives her possession of eternity.

Man is of the present, but woman lives in future generations.

On Prayer

"Speak to us of prayer," they said, and the Pray-er answered:

I do not pray because it is natural or philosophical to do so. I pray because I live.

I was made to grow. Desire accompanies growth; the greatest desire, propelling the greatest growth, is directed toward the Creator of life.

I pray to God for everything—not merely for my own happiness. I pray in order that the work of God may be fulfilled.

I believe that God will answer my prayer because I do not pray for self.

With Jeremiah, I would say that if God does not answer my prayer, it brings disgrace upon himself.

I wish—I desire earnestly—and I pray. But if He does not answer immediately, I am not dismayed.

I take it, rather, that God is postponing my plan—and I continue to pray.

To illustrate: four days before the tragic disaster of December 7, 1941, a group of us Japanese Christians kept a twenty-four hour prayer vigil. We knelt on the cold ground, warmed only by a charcoal brazier. We prayed for peace on the Pacific, and we knew that Christians on the other shores were also praying for peace.

Well, our prayers were not answered as and when we desired. But we kept on praying. . .

A Prayer

From the cruse of unlimited blessing, the oil rises and overflows. Thou alone knowest the mystery, our Father.

How oft I had fainted, except for thine cruse of unending grace. In Kobe's slums, in the barracks of Tokyo's settlement, Thou hast shown me as great a miracle as Thou didst reveal to Elisha.

Though I have never glimpsed thy face, I can see thy hand, pouring forth thy grace upon me—unworthy though I am.

It is a miracle to live in this age. All is miracle to me—being alive, walking, eating, sleeping, praying; the stalwart mountains, the silent grasses, the singing flowers; sickness and healing and health. A miracle even is death, the mower-down, for human life ever rises up again after his scythe has passed. The natural law itself is a miracle; I cannot fathom its depth.

The existence of conscience—what a miracle! Above all, the hunger of a praying heart!

Father, God, I pray without ceasing. Though I have not heard thy voice in human tones, I know that Thou hast answered my prayers—and more than my prayers. Thy voice differs from the human voice. Thou speakest through history and through the highest call of conscience.

Always I hear thy voice, O voiceless One, in nature and in conscience.

On Temptation

He, who early in his life had conquered the temptations to live comfortably, selfishly, and profligately, said to a youth who was similarly tempted:

The keener your life, the keener your temptations!
Tares, like wheat, abound in rich soil.

There is no temptation to those who are not conscious. To the blind, a fair lady is no object of temptation; and to the dumb there may be no temptation to speak falsehoods.

They who have no hands are not tempted to steal. The lame are not tempted to kick.

You see, the more your life abounds with sunshine, the more shadows of temptation there are. Beautiful and clever people often make the worst failures because their temptations to ruin are more alluring than those accorded to average people.

If you are an oak, do not wish to become a bramble in order to escape the winds of the heights. Develop the strength of the oak!

There is but one way to fortify the inner life, and that is to deepen your roots into the life-giving strength of God.

The day you wander from God, the Fortress Rock, all kinds of temptations attack and surround you.

As Jesus said, better to enter heaven with one eye than to be cast into hell with two eyes.

On Self-determination

To a man obsessed with the phobia that his every act was determined by alien, impersonal, mechanized forces, the Man of Inner Freedom declared:

Before we surrender to external determinism, we must fight the good fight of the self.

If we have to give up our ambitions and hopes because of weakness, or sickness or cowardice, we may be tempted to believe that life is controlled for us by nature, or materialistic determinism, or evil heredity.

But in spite of this three-fold determinism, we still have the freedom and power to open the inner windows of self toward the world.

As long as there remains the power of self-determinism through invention, discovery, and creation, I cannot believe that the determinism of the universe is fundamental.

When you give up the will to do good, there remains nothing but outer menace. As long as you voluntarily give even a small cup of water to the needy as he passes, you deny by that action that all life is determined from without.

We who believe in the inner light never fear the darkness of the world. As long as we determine our own lives in part, and retain a force or power to determine our own course, and keep the knowledge that our destiny is not ordered by the things outside ourselves, we need not be pessimistic.

Archimedes said, "If I can find a fulcrum for my lever I can lift the universe." So if we have the lever of self-determinism, we can lift the burden of the three-fold deterministic world.

You become a slave only when you take orders from an alien slave-driver rather than from the voice of inspired freedom within yourself.

On Immortality

When he was asked to give his ideas on immortality, the man who is destined to become an Immortal said:

Let us begin with certain truths of man as we know him. You and I have memory. Yet our physical bodies have chemically changed once every seven years. When we have lived fifty years; our bodies will have changed more than seven times.

But I have the same memory and ego; I am myself.

If I die, that is only another change. I will disappear from earth, but not from the love of God which has long enfolded me.

We came from the past, but in the past we had no reality. We do not complain of the time before we were born. God created us out of his memory to have existence here on earth.

So in the after-world, we shall still have existence in the memory of God.

We can have no real existence, either, here or hereafter, apart from God's power and love.

If we trust in God's memory through every universal change, we shall continue to have existence in God.

May God remember us!

If he remembers us, we can live by his grace forever.

If God says, "Kagawa, come out," Kagawa will come out to a fuller, better life!

Personal Atonement and Social Solidarity

He who, in the spirit of his Master, had so often taken the sins of the world upon himself, said to a class of Protestant theological students:

Modern society demands that we help carry the responsibilities of others—not that we are to interfere with their freedom or privacy when we are unwanted, but that we stand ready to interfuse our lives with theirs when they welcome our interest and help.

Society had become disjointed through many forces: jingoistic nationalists, class barriers, racial prejudice, economic competition, and professional specialization. The cells of what should be a corporate body, instead of working in unison, are shooting out aimlessly in all directions. It is our mission to charge those cells with unity and redeeming love that they may work together and bring adhesion to society.

There is no place in the divine-human scheme for the man who does not have the sense of social solidarity. He is an isolated, broken limb on the tree of human life.

One has to make amends for the wrongs and bear the burdens of others—that is atonement. Good society is impossible without the full development and expression of this redeeming love.

Many leaders of modern society are inclined to denounce the defects of others and to build society upon their own selfish desires. But Jesus' thought was always of all men. This is the fundamental principle of the organization of society according to Jesus.

Society which is not impregnated with mutual helpfulness must face disintegration.

The ideal society, like the man of love, must bear responsibility for evil as well as good in the whole social environment.

Giving and Losing Oneself

"How shall we think of giving?" the famed Giver of
Self was asked, and he answered:

Jesus proposed a new morality starting from the will
to live positively. "Be ye therefore perfect, even as your
Father who is in heaven is perfect."

To practice that high teaching we must learn to give
more than is demanded. When a selfish child asks for a
piece of bread, give him two pieces instead of one, and
teach him to share a piece with his sister.

When you do a favor for another man, do not think you
are doing it for him alone; you would feel a loss thereby.
Think that you are doing it for the organic whole of
humanity; thereby you feel no loss.

Society is organic. So to those who would borrow, it
is better to give than to lend. You should expect nothing
in return for helping a member of the organism of which
you too are a part. Does the hand demand a return in
kind for the food it gives the mouth?

If a part has been injured, we must try to prevent the
spread of the injury, and repair it to perfect condition by
double-quick action, partly for our own sake and partly
for the sake of others.

The idea of the Golden Rule is in accordance with the
principle of cell division, because to do for others is the
extension of one's self. Though the original cell be lost,
more than one comes to new life. The total result is gain,
not loss.

Jesus' saying that "except a grain of wheat fall into
the ground and die it cannot bear much fruit," is the
economic principle of abasement. In the economics of
life it is necessary to invest daringly, even though the
investment may be lost in the larger good. To walk two

miles when only one mile is demanded may seem like lost energy, but in reality it is a good investment. You have helped a comrade-of-the-road along his way!

To give to others and to forgive them is the way of the Cross. It is the way to perfect love. It is the essence of the will to save.

The Primacy of Spiritual Rebuilding

An American naval chaplain, having learned that about five hundred Protestant churches in Japan had been destroyed by bombing raids, asked the Japanese Christian leader if he would welcome gifts from American Christians to help rebuild the churches of Japan. Surprisingly, he replied:

Spiritual rebuilding must come first. Through repentance and prayer and divine guidance, we must build anew the religious foundations.

Unless a church edifice is a shelter for the Christian spirit, it is a hollow mockery of Christ.

Better that Christians worship with zeal among the ruins than that they worship by mechanical rote and ceremonial in a gorgeous cathedral.

If we continue instant in prayer and rebuild our spiritual life, the physical rebuilding of our bombed-out churches will automatically follow.

The homes of our people—ten million of them homeless—must also be rebuilt along with our churches. Our people can worship in homes, if need be, but not all of them can live in five hundred churches—though our churches have been used seven days a week for kindergartens, and meetings for social and spiritual advancement.

You ask me about the future of Christianity in Japan. I would not answer optimistically that it has "a glorious future," nor pessimistically that it has "a hopeless future."

Rather I would say realistically that the future of Japanese Christianity depends upon us Christians, laymen and ministers alike. It will take more than sermons to win people to our cause. We must lose ourselves in their welfare—clothing the naked, feeding the hungry, and sheltering the homeless.

Pray for us that our strength, through God, may partially measure up to our superhuman tasks.

The Seeds of the Cross

The Poet sang a lamentation to himself, and later to a few others who were inclined to listen:

Is there any spring, any springtime, in our lives?

The buds blanket fields with their beauty, but when shall the buds of the soul come to flower?

Love is lost in the streets, the lowly forsaken, as violence and greed run wild like wolves.

When, oh, when will the flowers bloom in the desert of humanity?

Friends, oh, friends, take up the plough, and sow the seeds of love.

How foolish to hope for the harvest of love without first planting the seeds!

This year, too, we failed to find the flowers in the field of life.

Plant and cultivate the spirit of co-operative love!

Then will come the day when flowers will blossom in the springtime of humanity, as in nature's springtime.

Then spring shall not pass us by; for, bending low upon this earth of ours, we shall plant the seeds of the Cross and water them with our tears.

Full Tide of Love

In yet another vein, the Poet sang another song that was like a prayer:

Rain! rain! O, gentle rain of love! We are wearied by the blood-rain of the sword. We must be cleansed by the flood of love that gushes from the Cross.

By the flood of this mysterious love, all the old dwellings of fear and greed are washed away.

All is borne away by the force of this flood of love.

Behold, it rises to the knees, to the waist, to the neck, yea, even to the crown of the head, until the whole man is submerged.

O friends! Are you ready for the flood which will blot out all tension between nations, and the friction between the colored and the white peoples of the earth?

For the adventure you need no Noah's Ark. Just plunge in bravely, and let yourself be carried away in its stream; national boundaries, color discrimination, economic exploitation—let all be washed away.

O, rise up, rise up, full tide of love!

Out of cold salt water, cold-blooded animals are born and warm-blooded animals emerge. Warm-blooded men, created from this new blood, must create a new society, in which love will overflow all distinctions of race and class, all false and narrow traditions. O sea, bring the purifying power of red warm love!

The time is now that the high tide of love, poured forth from Calvary long ago, should cover not only the seas but the continents.

The hour glass of my soul tells me that the love level is rising.

O Holy One, I feel thy heart beat in my heart!

O Love, I feel thy rising tide on every shore line of my life! *Amen.*

NOTES

"The Flame of Holy Ghost," page 20. This poem was written in Omaha, Nebraska, May 24, 1941.

"Prayer All Through the Night," page 21. Kagawa and several of his followers kept a twenty-four hour prayer vigil for peace only four days before the Pearl Harbor disaster. The above lines were written toward the end of the vigil.

"God Who Feeds Even the Fly," page 27. A note on Kagawa's imprisonment: Dr. Kagawa and his secretary, Mr. Ogawa, were arrested in August, 1940, by the Kempeitai (secret police) on the trumped-up charge of "placing the God of the Universe above the State." As they did not deny the charge during the speedy semblance of a trial, they were pronounced guilty. The judge made one concession to the Christian leader of Japan: he was led from the courtroom to the prison in ropes rather than chains! Kagawa and his associate occupied adjoining cells. They were not permitted to speak to each other, as they were in solitary confinement. They were on a slow-starvation diet but were not tortured. In fact, according to Mr. Ogawa, the warden treated Dr. Kagawa with unusual respect, addressing him often as "teacher." The warden was "almost persuaded" to become a Christian. Meanwhile, the Kempeitai announced that Kagawa had renounced Christianity—a falsehood they repeated several times throughout the war. Kagawa and Ogawa, after spending three weeks in solitary confinement, were released because Foreign Minister Matsuoka requested their release. Without that influential intercession in their behalf, their imprisonment would certainly have been much longer. Between 1941 and 1945, the books of Kagawa were confiscated by the police. He himself was thrice arrested, and questioned "many, many times."

"All Are Adornments of My Soul," page 30. This poem was written at the orphanage tent of Awa-hojo.

"Invention is the Gift of Heaven," page 31. This is the Labor Song of the Fuji Electric Furnace Company.

"The Day of Completion," page 32. Written after the dedication of the Tokyo Medical Co-operative Hospital.

"To Kagawa," page 39. Written aboard an American warship in Tokyo Bay.

"Who Shall Remember?," page 44. A poem begun on V-J Day, aboard the USS Missouri in Tokyo Bay.

"The Hedgerows of God," page 47. Written while sailing toward Saipan.

"The Anchoring Pull," page 48. Written in the Central Pacific, June 25, 1945.

"No Poppies Here," page 49. Written after visiting an American Marine Cemetery in the Central Pacific.

"Why So Class-conscious?," page 51. Written at Yokohama, November 13, 1945.

"Since Hiroshima," page 52. Written after a flight over the blasted city.